The Re

Di

The Reduced Law Dictionary

in snippets of 101 words

by

Roderick Ramage

BSc(Econ), solicitor

first published 2010

Published by

Etica Press Ltd
147 Worcester Road
Malvern
Worcestershire
WR14 1ET

A CIP Catalogue record for this book is available from
the British Library.

ISBN 13: 978 1 905633 10 4

Design and typesetting by Etica Press Ltd, Malvern

Printed by CPM (UK) Ltd, Poole

www.eticapress.com

preface

'If the law supposes that,' said Mr. Bumble,... 'the law is a ass—a idiot. If that's the eye of the law, the law is a bachelor; and the worst I wish the law is that his eye may be opened by experience—by experience.'

Charles Dickens,
Oliver Twist, chapter 51.

Hear, Hear! You respond. I, however, would be biting the hand that feeds me were I to endorse Mr Bumbles's claim, so instead, as a pension lawyer, I offer my thanks for the job creation scheme run jointly by the Department for Work and Pensions and the Treasury which keeps me in work, from which researching and writing these snippets is light relief. A few are mere anecdotes with a legal flavour, but most of are hard law, some prompted by my need to know what something means and other simply showing that the law and its clients can be asses.

(101 words, of course)

health warning

These snippets are not advice to any person (or at all) and may not be taken as a definitive statement of the law in general or in any particular case. The author does not accept any responsibility for anything that any person does or does not do as a result of reading any of them, but does hope that at least some of them will raise a smile. The date printed after every snippet is the date as at which (if at all) it reflects the law.

acknowledgment

Most of these snippets have been published in New Law Journal and others, I hope, will be in future issues. I particularly thank its editor Jan Miller, for not only applying the word 'snippet' to my 101 word offerings but inventing the title The Reduced Law Dictionary. See also the appendix in which, I acknowledge my sources, other than statute and case law.

about the author

Roderick Ramage qualified as a solicitor in 1966 after obtaining a BSc(Econ) at the LSE. His father has said that if he had no burning ambition to catch butterflies in the Andes, he might as well become an accountant, because they can always get work anywhere. He did serve six months articles to an accountant, during an enforced gap of one year to resit his second year degree exams, then switched to the law. In 1970 he published his first article in New Law Journal entitled "Will and Shall" about the use of those words in legal documents followed by occasional articles and law books (mainly Kelly's Draftsman and Table A, now Model Articles). His only foray into non-legal writing was a series of (unpaid) short stories in Lexicon, a small literary magazine in Stoke-on-Trent, where he was then in partnership in a leading local firm of solicitors. The editor of Lexicon complained that one story he had commissioned was too long: 'I only want a thousand words'. As about the same time Roderick heard a book review on Radio 4, in which the reviewer explained that the writer, who limited himself to pieces of 100 words, could not find an English publisher to take his work and so had it published abroad. On the strength of that Roderick rewrote his story for Lexicon in two versions, one of 1,001 words and the other of 101 words. There followed a string of 101 word snippets on motor cars and, mostly, human nature, until it occurred to him that his old friends at New Law Journal might be interested in (and pay for) the law in 101 words. They did, and here is the first collection of them.

contents

1   absurdity, doctrine of
2   adjustments for disability
3   annual leave and other time off
4   arbitration and human rights
5   augmenting the enemy's warlike force
6   bailment
7   bank security
8   BIS (formerly BERR) and Emerson
9   bicyclists on pavements
10   bread
11   bribing judges
12   casting vote
13   changing employment terms
14   cleansing pupils
15   company website disclosures
16   consideration for contracts
17   crime and criminology
18   Critical Mass, is it a procession?
19   cross-examination
20   death in service and TUPE
21   defamation
22   definition of beer
23   deposits and s94(2)

24 directors v shareholders
25 disclosing know-how
26 dishonesty is dishonesty
27 domestic emergency
28 drawing corks
29 dropped kerbs
30 Durham Fancy Goods
31 effective dismissal
32 elected by lot
33 employment abroad
34 envelope with name
35 European Parliament v European
    Commission
36 expanding the scope of discrimination
37 expressions of time
38 farming elephants in Scotland
39 final, conclusive and binding
40 flexible retirement
41 fraudulent and wrongful trading
42 garnisheeing bank accounts
43 grey squirrels
44 Hague-Visby Rules
45 have regard to
46 honest but mistaken belief
47 HR management
48 indentures and deeds poll
49 ject un brickbat

50 justifying dismissals
51 Kelly's Draftsman
52 landlords in repudiatory breach
53 law and plumbing
54 libel and chips
55 limited liability partnerships
56 liquidated damages in employment
57 mobile phones and the church tower
58 model articles of association
59 more nearly equal
60 moveable and immoveable feasts
61 notice periods
62 opting out of auto-enrolment
63 over promotion and stress at work
64 parties to a contract
65 pensions and maternity leave
66 performance not writing
67 permitted additions
68 photographing policemen
69 Pindaric Ode
70 police English
71 power of attorney by trustee
72 proprietors' own pension schemes
73 purposeful construction
74 R v Collins (1973)
75 references as qualified privilege
76 remoteness in contract

77 restrictions on the use of software

78 seat belts

79 Secretary of State

80 self-employed

81 self-intoxication and guilt

82 Sharia law and the archbishop

83 Sirius International (2004) - literal construction

84 slow track litigation

85 special notice (companies)

86 statutory assignment of chose in action

87 statutory maximum fine

88 stop on red

89 taxing directors

90 tenantable condition

91 termination of employment by mutual consent

92 TescoLaw

93 the Seneschal of Sark

94 thinking on your feet

95 trustees' discretions

96 under the hand of

97 want of consideration

98 whistle blowing

99 withholding consent

100 vexatious requests for information

101 yo

appendix - sources

absurdity, doctrine of

In Grundt v Great Boulder Proprietary Gold Mines Ltd (1948), CA, Lord Greene said that absurdity, like public policy, is 'a very unruly horse,' and arguments based on it should be applied with caution. This doctrine did not prevent the plaintiff, a director, from keeping his post, when, on his retirement by rotation, the motion to re-elect him was defeated. The company's articles provided that such a director would continue in office until the vacancy was filled or the number of directors was reduced; and no one was elected in his place and no resolution was proposed to reduce that number.

20.vi.09

adjustments for disability

If an employer claims to be exempt under s4A(3)(b) of the Disability Discrimination Act 1995 from its duty to make adjustments, it must, according to the EAT in Eastern & Coastal Kent PCT v Jocelyn Grey (2009) satisfy all and not just any of the four conditions set out in that sub-section, namely:

> (first) the employer 'did not know';
>
> (secondly) and 'could not reasonably be expected to know';
>
> (thirdly) that the applicant or potential applicant 'has a disability'; and
>
> (fourthly) is 'likely to be affected' so as to be placed at a 'disadvantage in comparison with persons who are not disabled'.

3.ii.09

2

annual leave
and other time off

Some North Sea oil rig workers, who worked two weeks on and two weeks off, claimed that their employer ought not to have specified that their annual leave was to be taken during the 26 weeks that they already had off, They wanted it to be taken in the remaining 26 weeks for which they were required to work. The Scottish EAT in Transcreen Resources Ltd v Russell (2009) rejected their claim. An employer can tell employees when their annual leave is or is not to be taken, but unscrupulous employers may not designate a series of weekends as annual leave.

6.V.09

arbitration
and human rights

M r Stretford held a licence from the
Football Association to act as a
football players' agent. In 2005 the FA
started disciplinary proceedings against
him in connection his acquisition of the
right to represent Paul Rooney.
Mr Stretford sought a declaration that the
disciplinary proceedings did not comply
with article 6 of the European Convention
on Human Rights (Human Rights Act
1998 Sch 1) to have his case heard by an
ordinary court. The FA obtained a stay of
those proceedings. An arbitration clause
can be a waiver of a person's rights under
the ECHR: Paul Stretford v Football
Association (2006).

16.xi.08

augmenting the enemy's warlike force

F oreign Enlistment Act 1870, s10 (extract)

'If any person within the dominions of Her Majesty, and without the license of Her Majesty,—

By adding to the number of the guns, ... or is knowingly concerned in increasing or augmenting the warlike force of any ship which at the time of her being within the dominions of Her Majesty was a ship in the military or naval service of any foreign state at war with any friendly state,—

Such person shall be guilty of an offence against this Act, and shall be punishable by fine and imprisonment, or either of such punishments.'

5

bailment

A bailment arises when one person gives possession but not ownership of goods to another. The leading case of Coggs v Bernard (1703) identified six classes of bailment, but Jones on Bailment (1781) identifies five: the gratuitous deposit of a chattel which the bailee is to keep it for the bailor; the delivery of a chattel to the bailee, who is to do something to or with it without reward; the gratuitous loan of a chattel for the bailee to use; the pawn of a chattel as a security; and the hire of a chattel for reward. These categories are non-exclusive.

24.xii.08

bank security

One of Stafford's jewels is the William Salt Library, now part of the County Archive. William Salt was a banker in the town. His bank became what is now Lloyds TSB. Not so long ago (I cannot remember where I heard the story) one Mr Salt, who banks at the branch which had once been his ancestor's bank, asked for a loan. 'Yes, certainly, but we will need security.' 'You mean some deeds? Yes? I'll bring some.' His ancestors had wisely kept the freehold, so within the hour he was back with the deeds of the branch itself. 'Will these do?'

3.iii.07

BIS (formerly BERR) and Emerson

In the Companies Act 2006, as most other legislation, the legislature tries both to micro-manage our lives and, Tartuffe-like, to delight in enacting what the law already says. Where does one start (or end)? Look at, eg, the bureaucratic procedures in sections 288 to 300 and then s282 saying what an ordinary resolution is. Yet, with wanton inconsistency, the Act says nothing about a matter so fundamental as how directors, apart from the first directors, are to be appointed. Perhaps BIS employs normal people amongst its robotic draftsman. Shout 'Emerson!' remembering his aphorism that consistency is the hobgoblin of little minds.

24.V.09

bicyclists on pavements

Darren Hall, who said that a motorist swerved and had forced him onto the pavement, sped round a blind bend on his bicycle and rode into Ronald Turner, age 84, who later died of his injuries. On 12 August 2009 the Dorchester Crown court sentenced Hall to seven months in jail after he admitted 'wanton and furious driving causing bodily harm', while in charge of a vehicle, contrary to s35 of the Offences Against The Person Act 1861. A bicycle is a vehicle: SI 2003/1101. There is no offence of causing death by dangerous or careless cycling under the modern legislation.

14.viii.09

bread

The Bread and Flour Regulations 1998, SI 998/141 stipulates that bread, which is a food consisting of a dough made from flour and water, with or without other ingredients, which has been fermented by yeast or otherwise leavened and subsequently baked or partly baked, and that flour derived from wheat, but no other cereals, must contain calcium carbonate, iron, thiamin (vitamin B1) and nicotinic acid, unless it is whole meal (or self-raising with a calcium content of not less than 0.2% or wheat malt flour) and iron, thiamin and nicotinic acid are naturally present in it in the specified quantities, not added.

5.vii.10

bribing judges

Once upon a time a farmer was in dispute with his neighbour. Before the trial of their case, the solicitor to one of them said:

'I am afraid your case is weak. You should accept the offer made to you.'

'That I will not, but would it help if I trussed a brace of chicken and sent them to the judge?'

'No. On no account do that.'

The farmer won his case, but instead of congratulating his solicitor, he bragged:

'It must have been that brace of chicken.'

'What?!'

'Don't fash yourself. I put the other chap's name on the label.'

19.vi.07

casting vote

Company statute law has had no problem from 1862 to 2007 with the chairman's casting vote at a company's general meeting, when the votes are equal, notwithstanding that the power can arise only on a motion which can be carried by a simple majority. Now BIS, with no judicial or other authority, has decided that a casting vote is no longer permissible, merely because the words 'simple majority' appear in the definition of an ordinary resolution in the Companies Act 2006 s282. Perhaps someone will defy SI 2007/ 2826 r3, put a casting vote in new articles and let the courts decide.i:

3.X.08

12

changing employment terms

You cannot change your employees' contracts unilaterally. If you do so, you risk that disgruntled employees will refuse the change and claim for unfair dismissal. You must have a good reason for the change and introduce it through a fair procedure, eg:

1 invite employees to agree;
2 consult fully;
3 warn that a refusal will result in a dismissal;
4 final warning;
5 notice of dismissal and simultaneous offer of new employment; and
6 implementation.

Stage 5 takes up to twelve weeks, say three months, plus two for stages 1 to 4, so you need about five or six months.

4.X.08

13

cleansing pupils

The Education Act 1996 ss 521 to 525 enables a local authority to have the persons and clothing of pupils at relevant schools examined whenever necessary in the interests of cleanliness and to have them cleansed at suitable premises, by suitable persons and with suitable appliances, if found to be infested with vermin or in a foul condition, and the pupil's parent fails to comply with a notice to cause the pupil's person and clothing to be cleansed. A parent may be fined if, after cleansing and through his neglect, they become again infested with vermin, or in a foul condition.

28.V.10

company website disclosures

By the Companies (Trading Disclosures) Regulations 2008, SI 2008/495, regs 6 and 9, made under the Companies Act 2006 s82, a company must disclose, not only on its business letters, order forms etc, but also on its website:

- its name;
- the part of the United Kingdom where registered;
- its registered number;
- the address of its registered office;
- if exempt from using the word "limited", the fact that it is a limited company;
- if a community interest company, the fact that it is a limited company; and
- if an investment company within the meaning of section 833 of the Act, that fact.

13.X.09

consideration for contracts

If you agree with another to sell him a car, cut his lawn or defend him in court and to accept some act or promise from him as payment, that act or promise is the consideration, It may be money, or other goods or doing something he was not already obliged to do or refraining from doing something he has power to do or any combination of these. Consideration must be real, but it need not be adequate: the law does not protect you from making a bad bargain. The consideration may be immediate or future, but may not be past.

25.viii.08

crime and criminology

Crime is what happens at 2 in the morning at the police station, when your would be client is in no condition to give coherent instructions, and then at 10 that morning at the magistrates', where his instructions are no more coherent. 'I wasn't there, but, if I was, I didn't do it.' Criminology is a way of exercising your brain in the glades of academia. Put it another way. What a criminal lawyer wants to know is whether Johnny actually did nail the cat's tail to the kitchen table. What the criminologist wants to know is why he did it.

18.xi.06

Critical Mass,
is it a procession?

Critical Mass is a mass cycle ride which starts at 6pm on the last Friday of every month on the South Bank under Waterloo Bridge. The police claimed that it was a procession of which prior notice is required under s11(1) of the Public Order Act 1986, and the claimant argued that it was not a procession because it had no fixed route. In Kay v Metropolitan Police (2008) the HL held that a fixed route is not an essential characteristic of a procession, but that by subsection (2) Critical Mass, as a customary procession, was exempt from the notification requirement.

15.xii.08

cross-examination

Never ask a question to which you don't know the answer. The defendant's barrister cross-examined a pump attendant from a garage, who testified that the plaintiff's sports car had pulled out of a side road and stopped at the lights while the defendant's lorry was still a long way off. The lorry had run into the back of the sports car. "If you are busy filling tanks and taking money, how did you have time to see what happened?" The question backfired and proved her credibility. She blushed and hesitated: 'It's the driver of the sports car. I rather fancied him.'

24.vi.o7

death in service and TUPE

Typically a pension scheme provides a death in service benefit, a lump sum of one to four times salary and often a pension for surviving dependants. As occupational scheme close, money purchase as well as final salary, the number of stand-alone DIS schemes has increased. By a quirk of translating European law into English (Pensions Act 2004, s255) a stand-alone DIS scheme is not an occupational scheme. Therefore a benefit which, if given in an occupational scheme, is exempt from transfer under TUPE, is not exempt if given under a stand-alone scheme. So beware of the grieving widow with her babe-in-arms.

20.ix.08

defamation

Defamation is a form of tort. A defamatory statement is one which has been made to a third party and disparages a person's good name or the esteem in which he is held. If it was in writing it is a libel and damage is presumed, but if it was oral it is a slander, which is generally not actionable without proof of special damage. The main defences to a claim for defamation are justification (ie, that the words are true), fair comment on a matter of public interest and absolute and qualified privilege. See the Defamation Acts 1952 and 1996.

25.viii.08

definition of beer

For taxation (not drinking), "beer" includes ale, porter, stout and any other description of beer, and any liquor which is made or sold as a description of beer or as a substitute for beer and which [is] of a strength exceeding 0.5% but does not include black beer the worts whereof before fermentation were of a specific gravity of 1200 degrees or more and "black beer" means beer of the description called or similar to black beer, mum, spruce beer or Berlin white beer, and any other preparation (whether fermented or not) of a similar character: Alcoholic Liquor Duties Act 1979.

12.i.09

deposits and s94(2)

The Law of Property Act 1925 s94(2) provides that deposits paid by buyers on property contracts may be returned in exceptional circumstances. Midill (97PL) Ltd v Park Lane Estates (2001) shows that we are still learning how that provision works. According to this case, it is not to rescue buyers whose contracts have turned sour. They must take the risk of market changes and, if they fail to complete, they forfeit their deposits and pay damages for any loss on the sale of the property. Section 49(2) is likely to help buyers only in cases on unconscionable conduct by the seller.

1.xii.08

23

directors v shareholders

Directors, not shareholders, have the power of management (Table A reg 70 and the forthcoming Model Articles, eg private, reg 3). A majority shareholder with under 75% of a company's shares, who is one of several directors, has no day to day power, except, with another shareholder, to requisition a general meeting to remove the other directors. It takes a couple of months or more to regain control. Morgan v Morgan Insurance (1993) was about costs, but came about because of just such a situation. One solution is to provide that directors' votes reflect any votes they can cast as shareholders.

25.ix.08

disclosing know-how

How much do you put on your website? Or hand out freely? I visited a client with my IP partner, who was horrified that I had handed my entire precedent employment contract to the client's HR manager. I told him what my publisher had said to me about making law articles freely available on the web. 'It's lifting your skirt to show an ankle,' he said: 'But you don't disclose the Crown jewels.'

The senior clerk at Queen's Square Chambers put it another way: 'You cast your bread on the waters and hope it will come back as smoked salmon sandwiches.'

17.iv.08

dishonesty is dishonesty

M r Salisbury, a former solicitor, was clerk to school trustees for which he was paid a fee. The trustees gave him a cheque in his favour, which he altered to increase the payment by £1,000. He was convicted for obtaining a money transfer by deception and the Solicitors' Disciplinary Tribunal found him guilty of serious dishonesty and struck him off the Roll of Solicitors, against which he appealed. The CA in Law Society v Salisbury (2008) upheld the SDT's decision and overturned the judgement of the Divisional Court, which had regarded the circumstances as exceptional and substituted a three years' suspension.

23.xii.08

domestic emergency

Harrison v The Royal Bank of Scotland (2008) does not help employers. On 8 December Ms Harrison's childminder said she could not look after her children on 22 December. Ms Harrison could not find a substitute, so she took the day off. The bank had told her that she could not have the time off and gave her a warning. The EAT upheld the Tribunal's finding that the warning was an unlawful detriment and rejected the bank's argument that the disruption of care arrangements must be sudden and unexpected. The disruption can be unexpected even if it is known weeks ahead.

13.X.08

drawing corks

Thompsons' website tells of two cases in 2008 in which they obtained compensation for unrelated clients, whose hands were cut by wine bottles which shattered when the corks were drawn. In both cases the wine was La Comida sold by Asda from an allegedly defective batch of bottles. Asda sells it for £2.29; but it is not listed by Addison's or the Wine Society. For one unlucky shopper, who required ten stitches and is permanently scarred, they obtained £6,000 compensation. For the other £2,500. Weren't we all warned of this danger (but not the compensation) when first introduced to handling wine?

2.i.09

dropped kerbs

If someone parks across your driveway without your permission and if you live in a special enforcement area (Traffic Management Act 2004 s84 and schedule 10) and if there is a dropped kerb to assist vehicles entering or leaving your driveway and if none of the exceptions apply (emergency services, local deliveries, etc), you could report it to your local traffic authority for the prohibition against such parking to be enforced under s1 of the Road Traffic Regulation Act 1984: Traffic Management Act 2004 s86. Alternatively, assuming that the Mikado's penal code is a defence, you could let his tyres down.

3.i.09

Durham Fancy Goods

In the good old days the Companies Act 1985 s349 (1948 s108) imposed personal liability on any person who signed a cheque, order for goods etc in which the company's name is not properly stated. In Durham a bill of exchange in the name "M Jackson (Fancy Goods) Ltd" was accepted by Mr Jackson without correction. The name should have included Michael, not the initial M. He was personally liable when the bill was not paid by the company. The 2006 Act s82 omits this useful provision, but regulations under it provide for a fine and s83 might help a defendant.

24.xi.08

effective dismissal

You read dreadful tales of teachers, NHS medics, the police and the like being suspended on full pay for months, even years, while a bureaucratic disciplinary process grinds its slow way to an uncertain conclusion. I used to ask employers whether they wish to please a tribunal chairman (employment judge) or do what's good for the business. Sometimes the best solution is to tell the employee you don't like his tie and frog march him off the premises, with a van blocking his car. The dismissal is unfair and in breach of contract, but the compensation can be a good investment.

25.viii.08

elected by lot

Election by lot has a respectable lineage, from the Commissioners Clauses Act 1847, s38 ('... in case of an equality in the number of votes ... the presiding officer shall decide by lot which of such persons shall be elected'), via such statutory measures as the Land Drainage (Election of Drainage Boards) Regulations 1938 s17, the Local Government Act 1971 s89, the Representation of the People Act 1983 sch 1 para 49, to the Greater London Authority Elections Rules 2007 regulation 53 ('Where ... an equality of votes is found to exist ... must forthwith decide between those candidates by lot').

4.vii.09

employment abroad

In Sayers v International Drilling Co NV (1971) an Englishman employed by a Dutch company under a contract written in American English was injured in an accident on an oil rig in Nigerian waters, and doubts arose as to the proper law of the contract, for want of a clause to the effect of: 'This agreement is governed by [English] law and the parties consent to the exclusive jurisdiction of the [English] courts in all matters regarding it.' For guidance on the territorial extent of statutory employment protection rights, see Serco v Lawson, Botham v MoD, Crofts v Veta Ltd (2006).

30.viii.08

envelope with name

An agreement for the sale or other disposition of land must be evidenced by a memorandum. The memorandum must be signed by or for the defendant and contain the names of the parties, the subject matter and the consideration. In Pearce v Gardner (1887) Gardner agreed to sell gravel to Pearce, which was on and part of Gardner's land. Gardner did not sell and Pearce sued for breach of contract. He produced a letter addressed 'Dear Sir'. It did not contain Pearce's name, but the envelope did; and the Court held that the letter and envelope together were a sufficient memorandum.

3.iii.09

34

European Parliament v European Commission

The Commission financed a proposal for a project that related to the security of the borders of the Philippines, specifically optimising border management methods, a system of IT, checking ID papers and staff training. The Parliament brought proceedings in the ECJ (Case C-403-05) to annul the decision on the grounds that the Commission had exceeded its powers under the regulation (EEC 443/92), which includes projects for such matters as the rural sector, food security, environmental protection, fight against drugs, protection of children. It argued that the regulation could not be extended by broad interpretation. The ECJ agreed and annulled the decision.

5.i.09

expanding the scope of discrimination

The EAT said that Mr English, who had suffered homophobic taunts at work, could not claim protection under the Employment Equality (Sexual Orientation) Regulations 2003, because he was actually heterosexual and his tormentors did not perceive him to be gay. The origin of their taunts was that he had been to boarding school and lived in Brighton. In English v Thomas Sanderson (2008), the CA reversed this decision. What mattered is not the victim's sexual orientation, but that he was the victim of homophobic taunting which created an intolerable working environment. This principle applies also to age and the other discriminations.

2.i.09

expressions of time

Unless otherwise agreed, "month" means a calendar month (LPA 1925 s61) and "year" is usually defined as a calendar year starting on 1 January, regardless of the number of days. It is better to say "four weeks" or "28 days" than "lunar month". A day is normally the period of 24 hours from midnight to the following midnight, but, in Cornfoot v Royal Exchange Assurance Corporation (1904), the apparent intention of the parties was that thirty days meant thirty consecutive periods of 24 hours and not thirty calendar days. A period "starting on 1 January" starts at midnight on 31 December.

5.xii.08

farming elephants in Scotland

The Disease Control (Interim Measures) (Scotland) Order 2002, SSI 2002/34 prohibits the movement of animals from the premises on which it is located, unless that movement is licensed under a specific or general licence by the Scottish Ministers. Specific exemptions include the movement of any pig in accordance with the Pigs (Records, Identification and Movement) Order 1995 and the movement of any animal direct from premises to a slaughterhouse. Animals were defined as 'cattle, sheep, goats and all other ruminating animals, swine and elephants', but by SSI 2002/ 369 for ', swine and elephants' there was substituted '(other than camelids) and swine'.

21.ii.09

final, conclusive and binding

According to Shell Egypt v Dana Gas (2009), QBD, the words 'final, conclusive and binding' in an arbitration clause were not to be sufficient to show that the parties had intended to exclude the right of a party to appeal to the High Court on a question of law under the Arbitration Act 1996, s 69. The exclusion of the statutory right must be clear, but need not mention the section. The failure to include an express exclusion clause in the agreement, prompts the suspicion that either none was intended originally or one part's intention was formed only after the event.

2.ix.09

flexible retirement

Normal pensions schemes may, since A-Day, permit their members, who have reached the early retirement age, to retire from the scheme and start their pensions, even if actuarially reduced, while not retiring from work. It might be a silly decision (getting less now instead of more later), but you are free to make it. Nanny NHS Pension Scheme thinks otherwise. First you must retire for at least 24 hours and then you must not return to work for more than 16 hours a week in the first four weeks from starting your pension; but it does create jobs for the administrators.

25.viii.08

fraudulent
and wrongful trading

Insolvency Act 1986 sections 213
(fraudulent) and 214 (wrongful). Both
apply in the winding up of a company and
a court order can make individuals
personally liable to contribute to the
company's assets. Fraudulent trading
applies to any person who was party to the
conduct of the company's business with
intent to defraud creditors or any other
person. Wrongful trading applies to a
director, who knew or ought to have
concluded that there was no reasonable
prospect that the company would avoid
going into insolvent liquidation and failed
to take steps necessary to minimise the
potential loss to the company's creditors.

18.vi.09

garnisheeing
bank accounts

Manchester's stype spoke at the local Lit & Phil. At the start of the War, he had been defending the NE coast. It would not have mattered if the Germans flying overhead had known that he had no bullets, as his gun was only a wooden mock-up. He felt much the same as a magistrate upholding law and order. But the Home Office had recently given them power to garnishee offenders' bank accounts. What the Home Office had overlooked was that few of his customers had bank accounts or even know how to get into a bank, except through the roof.

27.**X**.08

grey squirrels

The Grey Squirrels (Prohibition of Importation and Keeping) Order 1937 made under s10 of the Destructive Imported Animals Act 1931, prohibited the importation and keeping of the grey squirrel. While this Act dealt with musk rats, by s10, it extends the power of the Minister and SoS 'with respect to animals of any non indigenous mammalian species that by reason of their destructive habits it is desirable to prohibit or control the importation or keeping of them and to destroy any that may be at large' to make such order at they think fit to extend the provisions of the Act.

2.X.08

Hague-Visby Rules

In Jindal Iron and Steel and others v Islamic Solidarity Shipping (2005) the claimants, the sellers and buyers of goods carried by the defendant, claimed for damage to the cargo caused by rough handling. The defence, that voyage charterparty transferred responsibility for loading, stowage and discharge from the ship-owner to the charterers and consignees, was challenged on the grounds that the Hague-Visby rules provided to the contrary and that any agreement relieving the carrier from liability was null and void. The House of Lords held that the principle was long established that such a transfer of responsibility was not invalidated by the rules.

28.xi.08

have regard to

In Tesco Stores Ltd v Teignbridge DC (2009), Tesco, amongst other points, took advantage of the requirement in s70 of the Town and Country Planning Act 1990 for 'the authority [in dealing with an application for planning application] [to] have regard to the provisions of the development plan' to obtain an order for judicial review quashing planning permission granted to Sainsbury's, but it cannot be assumed that the directors of Tesco, in applying for planning permission itself, would have regard to a nearby owner managed grocery shop in accordance with s172(1)(d),(e) of the Companies Act 2006, except to take its business.

6.iii.10

honest but mistaken belief

Royal Mail closed a number of branches and transferred their activities to franchisees. It thought that the automatic transfer of affected employees under TUPE r4 did not apply, because it gave them the option of redeployment elsewhere or voluntary redundancy. Therefore it did not inform its employees' representative, CWU, that automatic transfers of employment would take place. CWU complained to an ET, which found that r4 applied to at least some of the employees. In Royal Mail Group Ltd v CWU (2009), the CA dismissed CWU's appeal from EAT's decision that the employer had fulfilled its duty to inform under r13(2)(b).

18.xi.09

HR management

'Nature has given women so much power that the law has very wisely given them little.' (Samuel Johnson)

A cocksure employee, who thought he knew the answers, explained to his boss why he was reading his magazine in the back office of a prestigious bank and, with confident bravado, suggested that we call today his new start. She, his boss, barely four feet ten without her heels, smiled sweetly at him and replied: 'Let's call this your last day.' He, six feet one and burly, trembled (metaphorically) in his shoes and slunk out.

No wonder so many women succeed in HR.

2.xi.07

indentures and deeds poll

"Indenture" has been obsolete from 1 October 1845 (Real Property Act 1845 s5, replaced by Law of Property Act 1925 s56(2)), but "deed poll" is still used, eg for a change of name. In time beyond memory a deed between two or more parties was written in sufficient copies on one parchment and cut apart with an uneven (indented) line, so that the separate parts could be authenticated by matching the indented edges with each other. A deed by one person (or two or more with a common intent) would be cut off straight with a pole to guide the knife.

29.viii.09

ject un brickbat

Law French was a dog French used in the courts as an artificial technical vocabulary. Some we still use (arrest, assault, attainder, covenant, debtor, demand, disclaimer, escrow, heir, indictment, joinder, larceny, merger, negligence, nuisance, ouster, remainder, tender, suit, tort, trespass, and verdict) but none so entertaining as the 1621 report of the prisoner 'condemne pur felony que puis son condemnation ject un brickbat a le dit justice que narrowly mist, et pur ceo immediately fuit Indictment drawn per Noy envers le prisoner, & son dexter manus ampute & fix al Gibbet sur que luy mesme immediatement hange in presence de Court.'

31.xii.08

justifying dismissals

In Boston Deep Sea Fishing v Ansell, CA (1888), Mr Ansell claimed that he had been dismissed wrongfully, and his counsel accepted that: 'if there was any circumstance which, though unknown to the company at the time they dismissed Mr Ansell from his position, would justify them in so doing, it was immaterial whether it was known at that time, and ... the company could justify the dismissal by proof of that fact.' However a dismissal can be fair only if the employer shows the reason for it (ERA 1996, s96(1)(a)), which must necessarily be known at the time of dismissal.

12.xi.09

Kelly's Draftsman

The EF&P contains the lot: the problem is finding what you want. Kelly, divided in to boilerplate etc, commercial, private client, land and not for profit sections, contains in each chapter (eg Employment, Leases, Commercial Contracts, Wills, Family) just about everything that a normal solicitor in a normal practice ever needs. Sorry, no aviation or marine law contracts or, securitised loans, but documents needed to form and run a private company and to employ (and sack) its staff. If you cannot find it in the EF&P look in Kelly. Even better, look in Kelly first.

But then I would say that.

20.ix.08

landlord in repudiatory breach

M r Hussein and others took an shorthold lease of a house from Mr Mehlman. The ceiling of a bedroom collapsed, making it uninhabitable, and the space heating failed. The landlord, in breach of the covenant implied by s22 of the Landlord and Tenant Act 1985, refused to make the necessary repairs. The tenants claimed that the landlord was in repudiatory breach of the lease, which they accepted by returning the keys and giving up possession; and the landlord claimed breach of contract. In Hussein and others v Mehlman (1992) the court upheld the tenants' claim and awarded damages against the landlord.

24.xii.08

law and plumbing

Resignation and righteousness are the twin emotions of plumbers and judges, who share the sadistic pleasure with which they survey the wreckage. Both meet their respective clientele when the latter are, in the case of plumbers literally and in that of judges metaphorically, ankle deep in water. Where the former asks 'Oh dear, who installed this? Had a stetson and spurs did he?', the latter animadverts on the infelicities of parliamentary drafting, the incompetence of contract negotiators, the folly or malice of litigants, the inability of lawyers to see the point and the other worldliness of academic commentaries. (per Seadley LJ)

23.xii.08

libel and chips

Slander consists of transient oral statements, while libel, is in a permanent (and therefore potentially more widely disseminated) form, even if the fate of newspapers, was to end as chip wrappings. The computer chip however should change the distinction. Whilst the Internet is widely regarded as ephemeral and unreliable, it is more or less permanent, including chat on social networks and blogs, which has often no more substance than oral statements. Defamation has a limitation period of one year from publication, which, with a paper publication, is what it says, but, on the Internet, it is whenever the material is accessed.

18.vi.09

limited liability partnerships

There are two kinds of limited liability partnerships. Under the Limited Partnership Act 1907, only the 'sleeping' partner, enjoys limited liability, but the general (working) partners remain personally liable. The Limited Liability Partnerships Act 2000 created a new form of legal entity known as a limited liability partnership, which is a body corporate separate from its members. It has unlimited capacity, but the liability of all its members is limited. Two or more persons carrying on a lawful business with a view to profit may form an LLP by signing an incorporation document and registering it with the Registrar of Companies.

17.xi.08

liquidated damages in employment

The Tullett company, knowing the difficulty and expense of recruiting someone with Mr El-Hajjali's specialist skills, stipulated in its contract with him that, if he failed to take up the agreed employment, he would pay a sum equal to 50% of his net annual salary and 50% per cent of the signing payment that the company had contracted to pay. Mr El-Hajjali changed his mind and did not take up the employment. Tullett was unable to fill the vacancy and sued for damages. In Tullett v El-Hajjali (2008) the QBD held that the payments were liquidated damages and not a penalty.

12.i.09

mobile phones and the church tower

A parishioner objected to a petition for a faculty to install a mobile phone base station and antennae on the church tower. The Chancellor concluded that some of the material to be transmitted through the antennae was not consistent with the Christian use of the church and dismissed the petition. In re St Peter and St Paul's Church, Chingford (2008) the Arches Court of Canterbury allowed an appeal to it against the Chancellor's decision. A balance must be struck between the public benefit (better reception for mobiles) and the risk of unlawful communications being transmitted, against which blocking techniques were available.

1.ix.09

model articles of association

A company must have articles. The
model articles in the Companies
(Model Articles) Regulations 2008, SI
2008/3229, will be the articles of very
company formed on or after 1 October
2008, unless other articles are adopted.
Except for alterations made to the 1985
version of Table A pursuant to the
Companies Act 2006, the articles of
association of existing companies continue
to apply to them, but existing companies
may adopt the new model articles. There
are model articles for private companies
limited by shares, ditto by guarantee and
public companies limited by shares. See
Companies Act 2006 sections 18 to 28.

31.i.09

more nearly equal

An employer's contributions to a money purchase pension scheme do not discriminate between ages, if they are at the same rate for workers of all ages. The employer may pay different rates according to the age of the members, if the aim is to equalise pensions for comparable periods of service (impossible to achieve) or to make pensions more nearly equal: Employment Equality (Age) Regulations 2006, SI 2006/1031, schedule 2 paras 10 and 31.

Obviously 99 is more nearly equal to 100 than 98. Unfortunately for equality it is equally obvious that 2 is more nearly equal to 100 than 1.

17.iv.09

moveable and immoveable feasts

The Calendar (New Style) Act 1750 contains Tables and Rules for the Moveable and Immoveable Feasts through the whole Year. Easter-Day, on which the rest depend, is always the first Sunday, after the full moon which happens upon or next after the twenty-first day of March, and if the full moon happens upon a Sunday, Easter Day is the Sunday after. As but one example of "the rest", Septuagesima Sunday is nine weeks before Easter. The fixed days are all Sundays in the year, 26 named days, Mondays and Tuesdays in Easter-week and Whit-week and the Evens before sixteen such days.

28.xi.09

notice periods

An unqualified number, eg 14 days' prior notice, may mean that there is only one day on which the notice can be given, but, if that is intended, it should, to avoid doubt, be expressed, as '14 days and neither more nor fewer than 14 days'. Otherwise the period should be 'not fewer (or more) than 14 days'. '14 clear days' means that fourteen days must elapse between the dates. Uncertainty whether the period is inclusive or exclusive of the date of the notice or its effect may also be avoided by words such as 'before (*date*)' or 'ending on (*date*)'.

14.xii.08

opting out of
auto-enrolment

From 2012 my employer must to enrol me into its pension scheme, and, if in the next 14 days I get through the hoops, I may opt out. Simplification (if that's what they still call it) says that I may opt out only with the correct form, prevents my employer from giving me the form, which I must obtain from the pension scheme, but I have to give it to the employer, who then deals with the scheme. Then, even though I stay with the same employer, I will have to leap these hoops every three years, maybe a dozen times.

22.vi.09

over promotion
and stress at work

Ms Dickins had been promoted above her ability. Her job involved preparing management and regulatory accounts and quarterly audits, which was at the limit of her abilities; and the promised support and training were not forthcoming. From March 2002 she told the management that she was at the end of her tether, asked for leave and for a less stressful job but later that year suffered a breakdown and left work before help was given. Her psychiatric illness was reasonably foreseeable as she had mentioned her problems frequently, and O2 had negligently failed to address them: Dickins v O2 (2008), CA.

30.i.09

parties to a contract

When analysing a contract always ask 'Who is who?'. Mr Brocklehurst, who carried on a hosepipe business, owed money to Mr Jones. He sold the business to Mr Boulton, but before the sale Mr Jones had placed an order for piping with the intention exercising a right of set-off. He refused to pay for the pipes so Mr Boulton, who then owned the business, sued for the price. In Boulton v Jones 1857, the court held that the offer was made to Mr Brocklehurst, there was no contract between Boulton and Jones, therefore Mr Jones was not liable for the debt.

24.viii.08

pensions
and maternity leave

Under s71 of the Employment Rights Act 1996, an employee on ordinary maternity leave is entitled to the terms and conditions (except remuneration) which would have applied had she not been absent. If the employee belongs to a final salary scheme, she accrues service during her leave and so her absence makes no difference to her benefits. If it is a money purchase scheme, her own contributions are based on her actual pay, so her fund will be smaller and benefits lower than had she not been absent. Not everybody agrees that the employer should pay the shortfall in her contributions.

20.ix.08

performance not writing

Equity can order specific performance of a contract, which is unenforceable for want of a written memorandum, if there is oral evidence of the contract, the plaintiff has performed some act of performance directly related to it and reliance on the lack of writing would result in a fraud. Mrs Wakeham, a widow, gave up her council house to look after an elderly widower in poor health, who promised to leave her his house when he died. She contributed to household expenses and received no remuneration. Specified performance to convey the house to her was ordered in Wakeham v Mackenzie (1968),

18.ix.09

permitted additions

Where an individuals or partnership carries on business in the United Kingdom, the Companies Act 2006 s1200 and 1201 require the disclosure of their names unless their business name consists of their surnames or corporate names with or without permitted additions, ie:

- for an individual, his forename or initial;

- for a partnership, the forenames or initials of partners who are individuals and, if two or more have the same surname, the addition of "s" at the end of the surname; and

- in either case an indication that the business is carried on in succession to a former owner of the business.

30.iv.10

photographing policemen

By s58 of the Terrorism Act 2000 "record" includes a photographic record. A person commits an offence if he makes a record of or possesses information of a kind likely to be useful to a person committing or preparing an act of terrorism, liable on indictment to imprisonment for a term not exceeding 10 years, on summary conviction not exceeding six months or, in both cases, a fine not exceeding the statutory maximum or to both.

You must have a reasonable excuse for, eg, photographing a policeman or a railway station if you are to have an defence under sub-section (3).

13.X.09

Pindaric Ode

In the interest of mutual respect, the following covenant is to be inserted in every lease of a Welsh residential property let to an English tenant.

x The Tenant shall, on each St David's Day, between the first and second hours after sunrise declaim the Pindaric ode entitled 'the Bard' by Thomas Gray in its entirety from a front first floor window of the Property in a manner audible to an audience assembled on the forecourt of the Property and [may do so either in the original English or (at the Tenant's choice) in Welsh (*or*) shall do so in Welsh].

19.ix.08

police English

Journalists and media types spend their time giving new meanings to old words and losing established meanings. Sure, they don't to it deliberately. It's a fashion thing without a moment's thought. The police are just as bad, except they do it solely by not thinking. They solemnly announce that a package or something is suspicious, rather than suspect. How then do they (and the journalists who imitate them) describe the state of mind of a person who suspects, eg, that the package is dangerous? Dr Johnson had the same sort of problem when he retorted: 'No madam, you smell, I stink.'

28.i.08

power of attorney by trustee

THIS GENERAL TRUSTEE POWER OF ATTORNEY is made on [date] by [name of donor] of [address] as a trustee of [name or details of the trust]. I appoint [name of donee] of [address] to be my attorney [(if desired) for a period of [x] months from [date]] in accordance with the Trustee Act 1925 s25(5).

date

Signed as a deed by [name] in the presence of:

Note. The donor must either before or within seven days after making the power give notice with prescribed particulars to the co-trustees and any person with power to appoint a new trustee (or as appropriate).

19.ix.08

proprietors' own pension schemes

An employer typically has power to remove and appoint pension scheme trustees and so power to :

1   change the deed and rules;
2   change investments;
3   admit new participating employers;
4   admit new members; and
5   refuse to permit early retirement.

If you have your own pension scheme and sell the shares of your company, you will lose control of the scheme, unless before completion you separate the scheme from the company (eg change the employer) or transfer all the employer's powers to the trustees. If you have no time to do this, the sale agreement must cover these points.

20.ix.08

purposeful construction

The application of TUPE to 'a person employed by the transferor ... immediately before the transfer' had been the subject of much litigation. Was the day before immediately before? Could two weeks before be immediately before? An employer, to accommodate the prospective transferee's wishes about which employees should be transferred, dismissed some employees before the transfer date. In Litster v Forth Dry Dock and Engineering Co Ltd (1989) the HL construed the 1981 TUPE to include persons dismissed because of the transfer, now done by the 2006 TUPE. However, Litster, no longer needed for 'immediately before', also gave us purposeful construction.

4.X.08

R v Collins (1973)

A girl awoke to see a naked man in silhouette on her bedroom windowsill and, believing him to be her boyfriend on an ardent nocturnal visit, beckoned him into her bed. When eventually she realised her mistake, she slapped him, and he fled. He was an opportunist who had seen her open window. He appealed against his conviction for entry as a trespasser with intent to commit rape and was acquitted because the jury had not been invited to consider whether he was a trespasser, which involved consideration whether he was inside or outside the window when he was beckoned in.

17.**xi**.08

references as qualified privilege

Qualified privilege protects a "character", given by an employer in good faith and without malice to a prospective new employer about an employee or former employee, from claims for defamation: Hodgson v Scarlett (1818). The parties have a mutuality of interest in the subject matter, but the qualified privilege may be lost if the communication is made to a third party. Therefore the "to whom it may concern" type of letters (these are properly called testimonials not references) must be very circumspect in what they say. All references should be marked "private and confidential"; and definitely not put on Face Book.

26.viii.08

remoteness in contract

Such loss 'as may reasonably be supposed to have been in the contemplation of both parties' (Alderson in Hadley v Baxendale, 1854) treats remoteness as an allocation of risk between the parties. Koufos v Czarnikow (1969) shows, that the contemplation test may rather be a method by which the courts can fill a gap by allocating risks not contemplated by the parties: 'The crucial question is whether, on the information available to the defendant ... he should, or the reasonable man in his position would, have realised that such loss was sufficiently likely to result from the breach of contract ...'

26.xii.08

restrictions on the use of software

Do not just click the I agree button, but read Apple's conditions when installing software to use iTunes.

'2. Permitted Uses and Restrictions. This license allow you to install or operate the Apple Software only on a computer system that came bundled with a licensed version of the Mac OS at the time of original manufacture. ... THE APPLE SOFTWARE IS NOT INTENDED FOR USE IN THE OPERATION OF NUCLEAR FACILITIES, AIRCRAFT NAVIGATION, COMMUNICATION SYSTEMS, OR AIR TRAFFIC CONTROL MACHINES IN WHICH CASE THE FAILURE OF THE APPLE SOFTWARE COULD LEAD TO DEATH, PERSONAL INJURY, OR SEVERE PHYSICAL OR ENVIRONMENTAL DAMAGE.'

4.i.08

seat belts

Lord Denning suggested that damages for injured passengers not wearing seat belts could be reduced by 25%, but nil if the seat belt made no difference or 15% if the protection was partial: Froom v Butcher (1976). In Gleeson v Court (2007), Gleeson did not wear a seatbelt, because the seats were occupied and he travelled in the boot. He also knew that the driver had drunk too much. His damages were reduced by 30%. In Palmer v Kitley (2008), the front seat passenger's damages were reduced by only 15% because the seat belt might not have reduced her injuries significantly.

26.xii.08

Secretary of State

Halsbury's Laws says: 'The term "minister of the Crown" may be used to denote the holder of an office in Her Majesty's government in the United Kingdom ... It includes, therefore, Secretaries of State, Ministers of State, Parliamentary Under Secretaries of State, and Parliamentary Secretaries.' The Interpretation Act 1978, s5, Sch 1 defines "Secretary of State" as 'one of Her Majesty's Principal Secretaries of State', which in any Act is the Secretary of State exercising the relevant functions. This convenient shorthand permits the legislature to be precise and accurate while keeping the legislated in ignorance of what they need to know.

20.X1.09

self-employed

Employment requires two parties, one who employs and the other who is employed. It is a relationship of master and servant, although nowadays few people like to use those words. A so-called self-employed person is not employed by anyone, in the sense of the law of master and servant. In particular he is cannot be employed by himself. He is an independent contractor who, in any work he does for another person, is employed by that person, in the same sense that one might employ a hammer to drive in a nail, but he is not employed as that person's servant.

15.vi.09

self-intoxication and guilt

'If a man, whilst sane and sober, forms an intention to kill and makes preparation for it, knowing it is a wrong thing to do, and then gets himself drunk so as to give himself Dutch courage to do the killing, and whilst drunk carries out his intention, he cannot rely on this self-induced drunkenness as a defence to a charge of murder, nor even as reducing it to manslaughter. He cannot say that he got himself into such a stupid state that he was incapable of an intent to kill.' Lord Denning in A-G for Northern Ireland v Gallagher (1961).

7.xi.09

Sharia law
and the archbishop

The law is multi-layered. If two solicitors disagree but one refers to page x in Kelly's Draftsman and the other concedes the point, that determines the law in that case. Either party could challenge it in court, where the outcome might be different, but mostly they do not. Similarly where parents set rules for their children, people form a club or adhere to a religion. They all set the law in their own context, but subject to national law. But the good archbishop who merely spoke of the boundaries between these laws was pilloried by the paparazzi and his own zealots.

11.ii.08

Sirius International (2004) - literal construction

'The tendency should therefore generally speaking be against literalism. What is literalism? It will depend on the context. But an example is given in The Works of William Paley (1838). The example is as follows. The tyrant Temures promised the garrison of Sebastia that no blood would be shed if they surrendered to him. They surrendered. He shed no blood. He buried them all alive. This is literalism. If possible it should be resisted in the interpretative process. This approach was affirmed by the decisions of the House in the Mannai Investment case (1997) and the West Bromwich BS case (1998).'

28.xi.08

83

slow track litigation

In 1994 the CA gave judgement in proceedings, Crown v City of London, started in 1613 by King James I, who claimed ownership of Smithfield Market. The judgement turned largely on the construction of a charter granted on 18 October 1638 by King Charles I to the Mayor and Commonalty and Citizens of the City of London concerning the site of Smithfield Market, following earlier charters of 1444 and 1505. The words "declare and grant" were apt to convey the land to the Mayor etc in fee simple, but the grant was subject to certain restrictions which were enforceable by injunction.

27.iv.09

special notice (companies)

Certain resolutions may not be passed by the members of a company, without special notice in accordance with s312 of the Companies Act 2008. Not less than 28 days prior notice must be given by a member to the company of his intention to move the intended resolution and the company must give notice of it to the members. Special notice is required of motions to remove a director from office (s168), to remove auditors before the expire of their terms of office (s553) and to appoint as auditor someone other than the retiring auditor or to fill a vacancy (s515).

25.viii.08

statutory assignment of chose in action

By the Law of Property Act 1925 s136 a legal assignment of a debt or other choses in action is effected if the assignment is absolute, in writing under the hand of the assignor (not purporting to be by way of charge only) is of the entire benefit, and written notice is given to the other contracting party. If any of these conditions is missing, the assignment cannot be a statutory assignment but is an equitable assignment, which means that the assignee cannot bring an action in his own name but must join the assignor as a party to the action.

19.iii.09

statutory maximum fine

Everywhere you look you come across 'on summary conviction, to a fine not exceeding the statutory maximum', but it took me over half an hour of LexisNexis frustration to find it. The smart thing, I can now tell you, is to begin with the Interpretation Act 1978 s5 and the words and expressions defined in Sch 1. It tells you that "Statutory maximum", with reference to a fine or penalty on summary conviction for an offence, in relation to England and Wales, means the prescribed sum within the meaning of s32 of the Magistrates' Courts Act 1980. In other words £5,000.

27.xii.08

stop on red

The Traffic Signs Regulations and General Directions 2002 tell us, in reg 33, the size, colour and sequence of illumination of light signals for the control of traffic and, in reg 36, their significance, of which the key passage is: 'the red signal shall convey the prohibition that vehicular traffic shall not proceed beyond the stop line,' with exceptions for the emergency services. The key point for the defence lawyer to remember is that the stop line can be several cars' length before the junction, so if you are in that space, you may proceed even if the light turns red.

29.viii.09

taxing directors

Directors are office holders, not employees, but their fees are taxed through PAYE as general earnings: ITEPA 2003, s5, s62. Schedule E is no more. Consultants, who as independent contractors bill companies and are paid gross, are taxed under Schedule D, are not happy if, on appointment as non-executive directors, their fees for their professional services change their character and are taxed through PAYE. Carefully drawn terms of employment will separate their roles and the method of remuneration for them. Their next headache is s688A, which might make them wonder why they bother to provide their services through their own companies.

12.X.08

tenantable condition

A covenant by the tenant to keep the property in tenantable repair might require him to put it in better condition than it was in at the start of the lease. "Tenantable repair" is the state which is reasonably fit for occupation by a tenant of the kind likely to take the premises, having regard to their age, character and location: Anstruther-Gough-Calthorpe v McOscar (1924). In practice the parties might be better advised to evidence the current condition of the premises in a photographic or verbal schedule of condition and for the tenant to covenant to maintain that state of condition.

26.viii.08

termination of employment by mutual consent

The claimant employee surrendered his keys, cleared his desk, said goodbye to members of staff and then made and lost a claim in an employment tribunal that he had been unfairly dismissed. The tribunal said that there was no dismissal as his employment had been terminated by mutual consent. The Court of Appeal in Walter Rodney Housing Association Ltd v Yaw Asamaoah-Boakye (2001) agreed with EAT, which had held that the employment tribunal was wrong to conclude that surrendering keys etc were enough to constitute an agreement by both parties on all material issues surrounding the termination of an employment contract.

20.ix.08

TescoLaw

In July 2007 the Solicitors' Code of Practice came into force and laid down that a solicitor's core duties are:

(1) justice and the rule of law;

(2) integrity;

(3) independence;

(4) best interests of clients;

(5) standards of work; and

(6) public confidence.

By and large we know all that without needing some bureaucrat to tell us. More pertinent is whether TescoLaw and other outside investors in solicitors will pay any attention. Of course they will emblazon the core duties in their publicity blurb, but in reality their directors will continue to perform their company law duty to maximise profits.

19.vi.07

the Seneschal of Sark

The Reform Law (Sark) 2008 permits the Seneschal, "an official in the household of a Sovereign", to be both a member of the legislature and the chief judge of the island. In R v the Lord Chancellor and others (2008) the CA granted a declaration that advice given to HM the Queen to give Royal Assent to the law was unlawful. The combination of the judicial and other functions of the Seneschal was inconsistent with the requirement of article 6 of the European Convention on Human Rights that the law must guarantee a fair trial by an independent and impartial tribunal.

8.xii.08

thinking on your feet

'Mr Wilkinson, before you address me, I should tell you that, where your clients' evidence conflicts with that of the plaintiff, I wholly disbelieve your clients.'

'Your honour. It does not matter whether my clients are world class liars. This is contract. Caveat emptor. The plaintiff, Manchester Garages Ltd, is a big garage. It has all the facilities and expertise to assess the car it bought from my clients, but failed to apply them. It cannot be heard to say that it was taken in by small time back street traders.'

Judge Bailey disagreed, but Mr Wilkinson's performance had been brilliant.

12.vi.08

trustees' discretions

Guaranteed Minimum Pensions are payable to men at 65 and women at 60. One question in Leadenhall Independent Trustees v Welham and Frith (the Maycast case) (2004) was whether pension scheme trustees, in applying part of a surplus, could in the exercise of a power, pay greater increases for male than female members in order to neutralise the discriminatory effect of the GMPs. Discretionary powers need not be exercised identically for all beneficiaries, but the difference in its exercise must be based on rational criteria as opposed to being arbitrary or capricious. The trustees could properly distinguish between men and women.

27.X.08

under the hand of

In Technocrats Ltd v Fredic Ltd (2004) Field J said: 'An assignment is only a legal assignment if it complies with s.136 of the 1925 Act. What that section requires is that there should be an "absolute assignment by writing under the hand of the assignor ..." ... none of the assignments ... was signed by Mr James personally; instead they were all signed in his name by his wife with his authority. Were those assignments "under the hand of the assignor"? In my judgement, they were not. ... these words ... require that the assignor himself should sign the assignment'

19.iii.09

want of consideration

Mr Beer obtained judgement against Mrs Foakes for £2,077/17/2, plus £13/1/10 costs and interest until paid. Mr Beer then agreed that he would not claim the interest if Mrs Foakes paid £500 immediately and the balance by instalments of £150. Mrs Foakes complied with the agreement, but Mr Beer sued for the interest. The court in Foakes v Beer (1834) held that he was entitled to interest because payment of the debt was not consideration. There was no new contract for the waiver of interest. Nominal consideration would suffice or the waiver agreement could have been by deed with no consideration.

29.ix.08

whistle-blowing

Whistle-blowing will probably get you sacked unless it is a "protected disclosure", when a dismissal would be automatically unfair: ERA 1996 s43A to s43L inserted by the Public Interest Disclosure Act 1998. To be protected a disclosure must be of failures of specified duties and be made in good faith to (so far as normally is relevant) your employer or a person prescribed under SI 1999/1549, with an exception for disclosures to other persons in the case of exceptionally serious failures. A disclosure to the local press detailing a potential hazard was protected in Collins v National Trust, EAT 17/01/06 (2507255/05).

3.X.08

withholding consent

Under the Landlord and Tenant Act 1927, s19, any provision against assigning, underletting, or parting with premises without consent is subject to a proviso that consent may not be unreasonably withheld. Landlords may prefer a bare provision against assignment, underletting or parting with possession without any reference to consent. The landlord may not refuse consent to achieve a collateral purpose unconnected with the terms of the tenancy: Bromley Park Estates v Moss [1982] 2 All ER 890. He may do so if the proposed assignee intends to breach the user covenant: Ashworth Frazer Ltd v Gloucester City Council [2001] UKHL 59.

19.ix.08

vexatious requests for information

The Freedom of Information Act 2000 s14 excuses a public authority from dealing with a request for information, which it considers to be vexatious. The information commissioner in case reference FS50157445/445 30/10/2008 supported the Cheshire Constabulary's refusal to provide information about its coat of arms and logo, and other matters. In Stephen Carpenter v IC and Stevenage BC (EA/2008/0046) the Information Tribunal upheld the commissioner's decision agreeing with the council that the persistent requester was vexatious and warned that in the future costs in significant amounts could be awarded. Updated guidance notes on vexatious requests were issued in December 2008: www.ico.gov.uk.

20.iv.09

yo

Pity about the 'Yo Blair!' and the sniggers which will colour your response to this piece. Studies by linguistic experts have shown that, from about 2004, pupils at middle and high schools in Baltimore have been using "yo" instead of "he or she". Previous attempts to create a neuter third person pronoun have failed. You cannot prescribe language, but an usage which seems to have arisen spontaneously, might just have a chance of success. If it succeeds, please do not rewrite Sir Charles Sedley's Parting to say:

> As freely as we met we'll part,
>
> Each one possessed of yo's own heart.

19.ii.08

appendix

Most of these snippets have their origins in the statute book and the law reports, but a few, mostly those for which I give my acknowledgment in this appendix, were prompted by articles I have read or, occasionally, real life

7 bank security

This story (not the William salt Library, which is a gem) might, sadly, be urban myth. I cannot remember where I heard it, but it is good enough to be true.

8, 12 BIS and Emerson, casting vote

No other commentator I have read supports my suggestion that BIS is talking nonsense by asserting that a chairman's casting vote at company general meetings is unlawful. Even if I am wrong, there are ways round the prohibition. My main objection is government meddling where there is no need: see the snippet on the cover of this book.

17   crime and criminology

With thanks to James Morton who wrote something to the same effect, but a whole one page article, in New Law Journal, Back Page sometime before (obviously) I wrote this snippet.

19   cross-examination

Told to me by Judge, then Mr Julian Hall – but not of himself. The traffic lights were on the East Lancs Road. In those days the sports car was probably an MGB or a TR.

24   directors v shareholders

All too often the law report tells you nothing about the real reasons for the litigation. I drafted the articles of associations in this case and my notes showed clearly that the late Mr Morgan, as a mark of trust in his minority shareholders, declined my advice to stipulate that votes exercisable by directors should equal the votes exercisable by them as shareholders.

25   disclosing know-how

In 2004 I organised a public meeting about the Employment Equality (Religion or Belief) Regulations 2003 for the British Chapter of the International Association for Religious Freedom, at which the speakers were Mr Paul Cadney and Mr Angus Halden from Queen Square Chambers, Bristol. Despite much publicity the attendance was five including the organisers. Both counsel and their clerk were very kind and understanding in response to my embarrassed apologies

40   flexible retirement

While the NHS Pension Scheme regulations do provide for a 16 hour week for four weeks on return to work, there is no authority whatsoever for the 24 hour retirement rule. In most cases the so called retirement is phony.

42 garnisheeing bank accounts

The stipendiary magistrate at Manchester was Mr Bamber, who was immensely entertaining, unless you were at the sharp end of his tongue

47 HR management

The bank is Coutts & Co, and the four foot ten boss is my step-daughter, Angela Wheeler.

51 Kelly's Draftsman

My editorship of Kelly resulted directly from some precedents I contributed to New Law Journal in my early days, so it was only fair that a snippet in the NLJ should publicise the book. My predecessor, the late Mr WJ Williams, was responsible for most of Butterworths' important equity titles, died suddenly. In their panic to fill the gaps, Butterworths gave me Kelly.